THE ART IN STEAM

BY THERESA EMMINIZER

Please visit our website, www.garethstevens.com. For a free color catalog of all our high-quality books, call toll free 1-800-542-2595 or fax 1-877-542-2596.

Cataloging-in-Publication Data
Names: Emminizer, Theresa.
Title: The art in STEAM / Theresa Emminizer.
Description: New York : Gareth Stevens Publishing, 2024. | Series: What is STEAM? | Includes glossary and index.
Identifiers: ISBN 9781538285442 (pbk.) | ISBN 9781538285459 (library bound) | ISBN 9781538285466 (ebook)
Subjects: LCSH: Art–Juvenile literature.
Classification: LCC N7440.E46 2023 | DDC 701–dc23

Published in 2024 by
Gareth Stevens Publishing
2544 Clinton Street
Buffalo, NY 14224

Designer: Leslie Taylor
Editor: Theresa Emminizer

Photo credits: Cover Poznyakov/Shutterstock.com; p. 5 Ground Picture/Shutterstock.com; p. 7 Pixel-Shot/Shutterstock.com; p. 9 Catchlight Lens/Shutterstock.com; p. 11 BearFotos/Shutterstock.com; p. 13 Anna Nass/Shutterstock.com; p. 15 4 PM production/Shutterstock.com; p. 17 ESB Professional/ Shutterstock.com; p. 19 Viacheslav Nikolaenko/Shutterstock.com; p. 21 Take Photo/Shutterstock.com.

Printed in the United States of America

CPSIA compliance information: Batch #CSGS24: For further information contact Gareth Stevens at 1-800-542-2595.

CONTENTS

Boldface words appear in the glossary.

What STEAM Means

STEAM stands for science, technology, engineering, art, and math. These different subjects share a common way of **exploring** the world. STEAM is about asking questions, thinking outside the box, and **solving** problems. Read on to learn about the art in STEAM!

What Is Art?

That's a big question with a bigger answer! Art could be painting. It could be storytelling. It could be dancing. Art is about creative expression. That means making something and sharing what is in your heart and mind with the world.

Visual Arts

The different kinds of art are called art forms. Art you can look at is called visual art. People who paint or draw are visual artists. So are photographers (artists who take pictures) and architects (artists who **design** buildings).

Literary and Performing Arts

Literary artists use words to create, or make, art. Poets, writers, and storytellers are literary artists. Performing artists use their bodies and voices to create art. Dancers, musicians (people who play music), and actors are part of the performing arts.

Artists and Their Tools

No matter what form they practice, all people who create art can be called artists. Artists use their **imaginations** to find new ways to share their thoughts, feelings, and ideas with others. A good imagination is an artist's greatest tool.

Artistic Skills

Artists need more than imagination and talent. They need **determination**. That's because creating art often means making mistakes. Artists must be ready to make mistakes and start over. Sometimes they do this again and again until they find what works.

Are You an Artist?

Do you like to draw or paint? Do you like to sing? Maybe you play an **instrument**. Maybe you like to put on plays. If you feel happiest when you're making something or performing, you may want to be an artist!

Imagine That!

You don't have to wait until you're grown up to practice art. You can do it today! The best way to start is by getting **curious** about the world around you. Strengthen your imagination by reading books or playing pretend.

Art Work

Working in the arts can be a lot of fun. There are so many paths to choose from! Do you want to be an artist? Asking yourself some questions can help. What **sparks** your imagination? What brings you joy?

GLOSSARY

curious: Wanting to know or learn something.

explore: To search in order to find out new things.

design: To create the pattern or shape of something.

determination: The act of deciding something firmly.

imagination: A place in the mind where you picture things or come up with ideas.

instrument: An object used to make music.

solve: To find the the answer.

spark: Light up or start.

FOR MORE INFORMATION

BOOKS

Bradley, Doug. *Writer.* New York, NY: Rosen Publishing Company, 2023.

Owen, Ruth. *Fold Your Own Origami Jungle Animals.* New York, NY: Rosen Publishing Group, 2022.

WEBSITES

Met Kids
www.metmuseum.org/art/online-features/metkids/
Learn about art history at the Metropolitan Museum of Art!

Smithsonian
www.si.edu/Kids
Spark your creativity with Smithsonian's fun activities, games, and projects.

Publisher's note to educators and parents: Our editors have carefully reviewed these websites to ensure that they are suitable for students. Many websites change frequently, however, and we cannot guarantee that a site's future contents will continue to meet our high standards of quality and educational value. Be advised that students should be closely supervised whenever they access the internet.

INDEX